Afterwords

Leon Weinmann

FUTURECYCLE PRESS

www.futurecycle.org

Published by FutureCycle Press
Lexington, Kentucky, USA

ISBN 978-1-938853-34-0

for Noah, Sam, and Ella

and

in memory of my father

But what must we actually do now, in our own time,
to reach timelessness, eternity, the marriage of
tomorrow-and-yesterday? Reason, he said, must prevail.
A bath in the aqua regia of intelligence must give their
true (primitive) meaning back to words, hence to things,
beings, occurrences. A tree must again be a tree, and its
branch, on which the rebels of a hundred wars have
been hanged, must again flower in spring.

Here my first objection came up. It was
simply this: I knew that anything that happened was
more than an addition to the given, more than an
attribute more or less difficult to remove from the essence,
that it changed the essence in its very being and thus
cleared the way for ceaseless transformation.

–Paul Celan,
"Edgar Jené and the Dream about the Dream,"
trans. Rosmarie Waldrop

Contents

Broken Ground

I

II

III

Acknowledgments

Broken Ground

All day, nothing

but frost, your spade, your hands,
the smell of raw clay bleeding
into the air like smoke. It hangs,
still waiting, in your throat.

All day, nothing

but the same repeated gesture, yielding
only fragments: split
sole of a single shoe,
cracked mouth of an inkpot.
At dusk, the plump half-moon
of a doll's abandoned face.

Still you are here, as silence

gathers like birds in the trees around you.
You will be digging here,
perhaps all night, clearing,
finally, a throat
for the mute earth, for the bones
that knock and knock against your blade.
You are waiting for them to sing.

I

Water/Zero

Chacun animal vit dans l'immanence comme l'eau dans l'eau.
–Georges Bataille

After the garden, the man and woman
squatted in a field of thorns.

See, they had become like us,
although they didn't know it yet,
knowing good and evil, which meant also

a whole bestiary of pain,
which was new to them, and so
in the infancy of their wanting

thirst and hunger, famine and drought
lacked at first their proper names,
settling slowly on their tongues
like sand blown through the teeth.

It took some time before they saw
that certain things were missing:
the beasts of the field fled from them,
the evening thrush was still.

And something else as well, a thing
that had no name, was missing too,
which had been everywhere before.

They began to speak of a *before,*
arranging stones to track the days,
circling them in the dry grass,
counting backward in their grief

to the first stone, day after day,
until there were too many stones to count,
and they built a house out of their grief.

What had gone? It was not in the sky,
or in the root, or in the wilted throat.
Before, it had been everywhere.

Above, the sky was blue and hard.
The leaves cracked in the wind.
They searched and searched the field in vain.

Only by digging an O in the earth,
carving and carving the shape of their grief,

did they find at last what they had lost,
and draw it up, and call it by its name.

Before, it had been everywhere.
Like nothing, it could not be
conceived. Now, in the sterile earth,
the man and woman made it into a thing.

And they saw that it was useful
for calling back the world,
the wild ass, the ox.
Later they found it could call forth
the green plants of the field as well.

But as with all the things that are
both intimate and necessary, they saw
how it could swallow and withhold:
the gourd dropped in the well.
The sea which never speaks.

§ 14

We can imagine how the first echo
must have terrified them,
their own voices in the well
calling back to them, their words
the only things that would return.

And so they kept the words,
and made themselves a song about the whole,
their small, round world, held out to hold
a place for everything that's lost.

Ultramarine

Outward and outward and forever outward

§

A hymn, an answer to,
such swelling: ringing back
at the broad-axe, oak,
the hermit-thrush still caroling
in the garbage-crusted woods.
A wish, to sing a single thread
through every leaf and eye,
returning each
back on itself again,
your great round closing
on its whole at last. O
a sum, for all our counting,
for all our lists, a word
would be success: only
there is no end
to this, this chattering
in desert nights, bad food and fever, cold;
always, we beat your continuous
song of incorporation, song of the gray
growing belly where we live.
Give us this last verse, a church, forgotten
in the fields, evening dying
on the doors; beneath the spire,
the instant of Assumption waiting
in archaic darkness.

If they came, we would be there, a lone
blue garment gasping in the sky.
We would explain all
to those who bore light.
We would lend grace to that last wall.

A Portrait

Here, there
is no place for you:

    your eye must wear out and turn
into a little brown wren, a sea
    of bramble and switch
        below you, no place
to rest, you will study
    me and learn
        nothing,
I will never be
    native land, I have
        no point
for you to claim as your own.

Worse, worse: you stand
    already in a foreign
        land, having
journeyed two days
    to see me, harried
over the black earth, lightless
    North Atlantic waste, suffering
the loss of all
    your markers, currency, down
frail boulevards choked with light

to this far wall, where
    you think
I have been waiting for you.

§

My maker was a drunkard,
   mad and mean;
      I knew him not,

knew neither the peerless
   truth he sought
      to paint on my breast

in precious ultramarine;
   to his sorrow,
      I was not

his child, I refused to sing
   for him, I was unable
      to free him from his marked skin,

and so he abandoned me.
   I hang
      between disgrace

and triumph still,
   martyr or whore. They say
      I'm a superb example

of his early style, the clear
   vision that he once pursued
      and to which you now return.

§

Pity, Traveler,
    the eye, unanswerable,
        given

to our kind— I am, for you,
    a landscape without figures,
        a cropped swath of ragged weeds,

then, lost
    in some grass, a thin
        light crying

out to no one. It says
    I will not be yours.
        It says

bramble.
    It says
        switch.

In Doubt, Recalling Cordelia

I cannot heave my heart into my mouth.
Or one hundred-eighty swallows turning south,

or the hen-and-chickens clustering on the garden wall.
That is not all: I cannot tell you all

the scroll of steam uncurling from the tea
might say about what is, or what might be,

the common bloodline of this apparent world.
Its speech is locked away, a furled

flag of an antique country, since just a minute ago
was autumn, you saw it, the gold funeral fires, the smoke, and now

come these white billions, already, each irreplaceable flake,
and there is just too much to say for them—to say it would take

a tongue as old, as young, as Alexander, for too much goes
unnamed, unnoticed, more is coming, it snows

and snows all day and night and buries all the words.
But we are still responsible for them all, responsible for the birds,

the burning leaves, the climbing vine, we are the only ones
who can say just what it is we saw. And progress swells, a new
    scene runs,

and still we drop our lines, forget,
the silence piles up in drifts, we let

the words get lost, the tongue stalls—
How can I say how I love you? The burden of the old tune falls

out of my mouth like a stone. And do we name them cursed,
   or blessed,
who love according to their bond, no more, no less?

Theogony

First they raped him, then they made him sing.
Before was neither
paradise nor the idea
of paradise, and time
was distant, groaning on the deep.

He couldn't have told us then: nothing
happened, nothing stopped
happening—above, the sun, still putting out
the eyes of the white sea-cliffs; the sea,
still sucking at the garbled shore.

Lightheaded, shepherd Hesiod,
driving once again up Helicon his flock,
the rich, pellucid wool,
glancing white, red, bright
freshet of blood and sperm,

might have worked it into tune,
quickening leaves, clacking
tusks in the panicked brush,
thunder shaking the olives down,
but he had no sense of time.

And then the Muses
taught him song, twisted
him into their belly, sack
to empty, fill with truth,
with falsehood, as they wished.

The zero hour, noon, and no one
near, just tree limbs knocking out
a meter in the middle of the air, and time

wrapped itself in ribbons of wool
around the olive branch they made him hold.
He spread his mouth, the gods came in and out,

he choked on swansdown, bryony, blood
of the god, sea-foam
of heartless Aphrodite, hot
bronze of the new-forged shield
burning his swollen lips.

Tasting all these things,
he spit them out in song,
and they were gone.

Time remained. Passed.
He wiped his bloody mouth.
Already, over the sea,
new things were happening,
the Scamander clotting,
fire billowing below decks, in the dead lungs.
Already other songs were being sung.
Already men wanted something back.

§ 24

Exercises with Fermata

1.

Silence is your theme.
Your method: compare

silence to a secluded pond.
Suggested words:
plunge, breathless, heart.
You might mention
the quality of light as well.

2.

Another approach.
Certain lines
may echo for you here:
Nothing beside remains.
Oed' und leer das Meer.
Inaudible as dreams.
Avoid like or as.
Refrain

3.

Now
open your Sappho
her ragged erotic

lacunae her beautiful
holes so true so
un[ ]able.
But all must be endured, since

4.

Strike *true,*
strike *your.*

Repeat.
Rest.
Repeat.

II

Middlesex Pastoral

The boy has had a fever for a long time.
He lies in a dark room full of dreams.
At dusk his father tries to make him laugh
and drags their billy goat up to his bed.
The boy can't say if this is real or not.
All afternoon he has been swimming down
a stream of ash and thorns to find himself
in what is either his own bed or else
another strange room far away from home.
The father, or the dream who looks like him,
gives the boy some water. He shuts his eyes,
slipping again into the stream of ash,
dreaming that he hears the goat on the stairs,
the scared hooves beating against the plaster.
Only later, when he can walk, and sees
the mark of the cleft in the wall, does he
remember the cleft between the real world
and the world in his room full of dreams.
One night the little girl next door brings him
a gift to soothe his fever, a tin fire truck
with a working ladder and spinning lights.
He should remember, but that night he flies
to every city of the world in that truck.
Later, when he loses the truck, he wonders
if it was another one of his dreams.

§

Now the father's hands are breathing smoke.
The boy is better, and expected to work.
In the barn all day he has been stacking up
the green wood for the winter-time; now he stands

to watch his father drop the veil over his face,
then feed a fist of hay into the belly
of the burning smoker. Ready now, the father
strides up the hill to his five white hives.

The ancients believed that bees were ruled by a king;
the father knows the truth, but it does not matter,
he knows he is a strange white god to them,
and when he lifts a frame and blows his smoke
they drop like raptured worshipers.
From a distance, the hives are meetinghouses,
two hundred thousand praying stingers tuned
like compass needles, hymning their one desire
into their blank animal deafness.
The order of their world is a marvel,
proclaims the father, descending to the barn.
The air around him sings with heat.
The stubble in the smoker writhes and cracks.
The boy notices that a few bees have sheltered
in the father's beard, the beard of their god.

§

Days later, the father and the mother harvest honey:
Against the peeling clapboards, bubbling glass,
the bees swarm, heaving like a lung
in the hay-colored air, a braid of sound and light.
The father and the mother do not know,
though they suspect, this is the last harvest.
Distance hums between them in a current.
Still, they seal the jars in silence, case by case,
ignoring the bees that cluster everywhere,
twitching on the mantel's passive photographs.

The boy hides in his room and still gets stung.
They give the boy a piece of honeycomb.
At night he wonders if it is the bee
that makes the comb or the comb the bee.
He dreams of angry bees in his mouth.

§

Each morning the father brings the mother
a bee held out in tweezers like a jewel:
its sting is said to ward off illness. Yes,
there once was a boy, somewhere in Europe,
who was stung a thousand times when he was only
two weeks old. That boy, the father says, that boy
was never sick a day in his life.
The boy imagines swollen lips and eyes.
The father plucks the stinger out and brings the ice.

§

Now the rain comes down: the boy dreams water
is eating the house. He remembers Noah,
works to picture the impossible
end of the world, white nothing. Black nothing.
In his room, the rain ticks in a pail,
measuring out the dark and then the light.
The bridges break, the lights go out,
a stream has carried the road away.
The parents also leave for days and days.
A woman whom the boy has never seen
stays at the house. She takes him on her lap
and tells him things he cannot understand:
the mother has broken the water,
has gone to deliver a baby,
has lost the baby somewhere on the way.

The boy drifts in the woods and finds
a dozen wooden horses that have washed there
in the flood. They are not what he was looking for,
but he picks them up and carries them back home.
The horses are no bigger than his palm, black, white,
all of them blind, the jeweled eyes drowned.
He keeps them in his room that night,
then sets them in the stream that was the road.
Black, then white, then black, they ride away.
The boy remembers, knows that they were real.

§

But now there is work to do, and remembering
is not it: leaves have fallen
everywhere and need to be removed.
The boy and the father rake them in
and burn them in a trough. Fall down: fall up.
The mother has not spoken in so long
the boy no longer knows her voice.
She sleeps, grows thin, her long hair short.
They burn more leaves. Fall up. Remember each one.

§

All the stories in church are about things
that disappear and then come back again.
Gone for months, they sit together in back
and listen to a story they all know,
how in the beginning there was only
water, with a spirit sailing on it,
then land and plants and animals and man,
and then just a little while later
everything returned to water again,
until the land and plants and animals

returned as well, and man also returned.
Noah and his family had to make
new barns and houses, roads and fields and towns.
Each thing that came back became the first thing.
It has been a warm fall, and when they leave
they notice that the grass is growing still
though the leaves have been gone for many weeks.
They eat lunch in town, and the mother laughs
when the boy repeats the minister's joke
about how Jesus likes to play doctor.
He had said to her, *Little girl, get up!*
And that man had seen what looked like trees, walking.

Later, driving home, the boy sees how
the town has changed its face: the Pattaconk's
back room has slipped away into the Sound;
the hardware store is a coffee shop.
The air is full of earth and new wet wood.
A small voice in the front seat is humming
about the weather, sun and rain, frost, then snow.
The father and the mother do not speak,
though twice they take the other's hand and squeeze.
Their smoke embraces awkwardly between them.
Pale in the pale sky, the moon's white eye
is following them home, waiting for night.

When they get home, their driveway is a stream
of red and yellow flashing lights that splash
and burn against the barn and the white house.
Your neighbor called, the fire marshal says,
then points up to the beehives on the hill,
where three yellow firemen stand around
a capsized hive, and then, beside the hive,
the swollen body of the billy goat,

the silken beard upturned, the tortured horns
dug in six inches into the sodden earth.
Bees and light and crackling voices
draw circles over his open mouth,
around his crusted honey-colored eyes.
And there is nothing they can do, and so
the father takes the goat and buries him
in the crush of bramble under the back wall.
He finds two arrowheads, and the headless
torso of a tiny porcelain man,
and rinses them, and gives them to the boy.
His eyes are gold coins now, washed in mud.
His horns are curled in the wet clay like snails.

§

And then, next week, the hives are gone as well,
and in their place the boy finds only
brown squares thick with sightless bugs and worms.
And then it snows, and the worms are also gone.
And then that winter, when the boy keeps dreaming
that the earth is one black ball of ice,
that snow is growing out of the ground,
rootless, orphan flowers, the mother
disappears as well, to a distant road,
a small apartment with a balcony
looking out over a strange white city.
The father kneels before the stove,
feeding and feeding trees into the fire.
The boy sits in the kitchen writing letters
on the ice inside each windowpane,
then watching as the stove burns them away.

§

Mornings the boy goes out to the back field
and looks for things he hasn't seen before.
In February he finds a little fox
dead in the thorns, its neck filled up with snow.
In March an ice storm holds the field still;
he plucks the glassed-in winterberries,
holding them till they bleed in both his palms.
In April, in the rotting apple tree,
a snakeskin and a broken robin's egg.
He brings them back at night to the quiet house
and lays them on the empty mantelpiece.
For months there has been no work for him to do.

By early June the field has grown rank:
against the back wall's bramble, the stinking
trees of heaven crowd, the sumac swells
its clotted lungs for the yellow jackets,
and flowers whose names the boy does not yet know
rise up against the first heat of the year,
heal-all and lamb-kill, goat's-beard, bee-balm,
birth-root and cancer-root, bitter-bloom, rue.

In August, when the boy is finally told
that he must leave the house and town as well,
he goes out late one night into the field
to lie down in the high and canting grass.
Over his head, heat lightning flares and dies,
the last fireflies blink and disappear.
Lots of things are busy going away.
The boy thinks hard and tries to remember them.
Behind the house, already, he can hear
the first green walnuts dropping to the ground.

The Collar

But we do be afraid of the sea, and we do only be drownded
now and again.

§

This is what they told me once.

The man and his pregnant wife
went out for an evening swim.
Over the blue hills, the moon,
a faint pink egg, suspended;
the water, smooth as a veil.
Late August, '72.
They were sort of happy then.

How late that night, on the sand,
the man bent over to lay
his ear on her warm belly,
waiting for the sound: the new
straining of oars, the strange new
amniotic choruses.

How the next evening they learned
about his naked body
pulled out of the same water,
the anonymous young boy,
arms bound hard behind his back
with fishing line, the same line
corded deep into his neck.
How all that lovely evening,
silently, under their feet—

How the woman wept, afraid
this was an evil omen—

she'd lost a child already.
She would be mistaken—still
this is what she thinks about
when she thinks about water.

§

If you ever go fishing
in the Quabbin Reservoir,
in central Massachusetts,
you will be able to see
the remains of entire towns:
long stone walls drowning themselves
patiently along the banks,
the foundations of houses,
churches, all the empty streets.
People haul up some strange things—
railings, farming tools, teapots.
Once I pulled up a long chain,
and at the end, the twisted
collar of an animal,
and I remembered the boy.
Police identified him
but I never learned his name.

Last summer, our son Noah,
six, nearly drowned when he snagged
his hair in the cracked helix
of a metal ladder wrecked
on the bottom of a lake.
When we pulled him up he looked
like a son I'd never had.

I kept that collar for years
before it pulled asunder.

I can still draw each link up,
one by one, remembering,
but when I get to the end
there is only myself, here,
October, in this inlet
where the fish don't swim, the wind
won't blow, where the weak sun dies
in the brittle trees, and where
whatever still is is still
suspended over the wide
open mouth of the water,
waiting to be bound away.

§ 38

Korē

You know a symbol when you see
one: nothing
in the world so blue
as the blue narcissus, the dark
blue narcissus nodding
from the field's ragged edge.

Behind, the endless orchard, the blood-
hot plums flooding themselves.

In the photograph, her eyes
are shut, her face
a magnesium flame.

Behind, her shadow,
face down in the grass.

In the beginning there had been
no God, or God
was everywhere, she doesn't know.

§

Her mother will keep the house.
Her father takes the crystal, saying
I intend to do a lot of entertaining.
The fire stumbling in the wind.
The back pond scabbed with early ice.
It's true the earth
split open like a seed.

§

She sits in her father's study
rereading the Oedipus cycle.
The air is calfskin, pumice.
The page is lightly foxed.
He watches her read.
You know a symbol when you κτλ.

Korē, the Virgin,
mistress of the dead
tongues, pulls back her hair,
puts on a turtleneck.
The *Oedipus Rex* is a veritable
treasure-house of grammatical peculiarities.

§

Back for the summer, she sees her mother
has lost some weight, bought some clothes.
Around her, throngs of men,
wallets full of sacrifice.

Her mother buys a pregnancy test.
All things come into being
through strife—cell
divorcing cell, the flesh
dividing against itself.
Who are we now?

Two nights later, she herself
(herself) will lie
in a humid grove, half-drunk,

a slip of a boy mouthing
adjectives at her. She is X, she is Y.
Goddess of corn, Queen of the dead.

§

Fall once more, the cell divides again.
She sits in her father's study
rereading the Oedipus cycle.
You know a symbol when you see one.
X, Y, always here, there.

Lethe

In dying spring the flood
was our relief. Remember:

each dawn swollen like a bruise,
the vaulted sky a tarnished spoon,
silences quarreling in our throats.

Watching, from our separate rooms,
the warm air thicken with deserting birds,
the foreign water swallowing the roads.

An act of kindness: a large world
made a little smaller.

§

Smaller still. Soon we could no longer
say, "Here is the table. Here,
the couch, exactly where we left it.
Here, our bed, still squarely on its legs."
It makes no sense at all

to say, "You may" or "You may not
come in." The door, bared
to the ravishing waters, giving
no refusal or response.

§

Or how, having been resolved,
you stepped into the narrow boat
and drew your marble arms along the bow.

Contagion all
about your brow,
a wreath of smoke.

Raise your eyes to the other bank.
Bind yourself away, across
such wide misery, into forgetting.

To His Soon-to-Be Ex-Wife, Imagined as a Meadow

As a lantern in a field calls out

moths, the white sheets
   torn like shipwrecks
      on the light, the listing
grass, assuming
   slowly, slowly
      their alien snow,
my eyes, awake
   on your sleeping hip
      (as under
the moon a low
   hill loses
      its dark), summon
another loss, pull you
   from me utterly, away
      from what you were. Now—

§

God, I want
   to be satisfied by you,
      so much, too much,
more than enough, I know.
   It is not enough
      to shut your eyes, your ears
still hear
   the crickets, frogs, the crowded night
      singing, you can smell
the new-cut timothy, still
   the wet pines settling
      on sheet, on skin, no end.

§

Orpheus, Lot—they learned
    how merely our presence
        in a field kills the field,
the plow's strophe,
    the eye's blade pruning back
        fullness.
What you want (remember
    this) is not what lies
        beside you. You want
to know what the field is doing
    in your absence,
        how it survives
apart from your senses, its roots, nerves.
    No. I want you—
        wholly, but even naming this,
the world itself, lit up
    before us as a form, seems
        only the lantern, only
another kind of dying.
    It is the mountain hidden
        in the teaspoon, dark
matter, presence denying
    our taking in
        that haunts. That's why
we invent ghosts, the longing for witness,
    the dream of our own presence
        culled of form.

§

Here, now:
    we both need this
        to be enough, two definite
bodies meeting in eclipse. Stare at it
    too long and it is not
        the eye but the sun itself
that burns out. That's what they say
    in the myth, that when he looked
        over his shoulder, spoke
her name, his
    love fell into
        a dark so heavy
even a lantern wasn't enough
    to help him find his way across
        that asphodel to her again.

The Infants

for X, b. 5/30/71, d. 5/30/71
for Y, b. 7/21/75, d. 7/21/75

Let death a warning ever be,
That you all walk a troubled sea,
The waves of death how fast they roll,
To waft away the weary soul into
eternity.

I thought maybe I'd find you here today,
in the crooked stone beds of these fathers,
weird, bearded men and their mute consorts,
some praying angels, here and there an urn,
and the sky an antique pewter bowl,
the last brown leaves falling predictably.

Death is a debt to nature due
Which I have paid and so must you.

Though I never knew you, no one knew you,
and I can't really care about you,
I was wondering what they said about you
then, when they let you down with the grown-ups,

It may truly be said
He was a GOOD MAN

...

Her ways were ways of
PLEASANTNESS

...

or if they gave you anything to say—

Life's boisterous scenes are past away!
Its joys with me are o'er

...

Let this vain world engage no more:
Behold the gaping tom[ ]!

but I have looked and I can't find you here.
Maybe you are buried somewhere else,
or drunken teens have swiped your little stones,
or the grass and moss have overgrown you.

No—

I know I'm deceiving myself. I know
that infant stones, like infants, do not speak.
And still I'm here. I'm here because
I'm here and you are not.

§

When lingering pain her bosom tore
Resigned she kissed the chastening rod

If you could think, I'd have you think of this.
Our mother slumps all night now in her chair,
curled up with her purses of narcotics,
her Marlboro 100s, Diet Coke,
her cats who have grown wild in the house;
the TV bends above her in her sleep
to flicker over her bewildered head
sweet, nothing, its forked and glittering tongue.
Her spine's been trained in the shape of the hurt,
a question mark of spurs without a point.

You two, as chiseled serifs which are made
by carving their own absence on the stone
have on her written your own elegy.

§ 48

§

As you are now, so once was I,
Rejoicing

It's hopeless, and it's getting dark.
A thin mist twitches in the crotch of an oak.
And I know that I won't find you,
though I think you must be
somewhere, past this horizon,
where the narwhal rides the blue-black sea,
where the buck sheds horns in the bramble,
where the traffic drones on the Long Island Expressway.
Somewhere tonight, in the atoms of man and earth,
your empty veins curl up among the roots;
your small red hands, long gone
from sight, still grasp the clods
of the freezing, fertile soil.

    in my bloom;
As I am now, soon you must be,
Dissolving

§

The fathers and their faithful relicts
crumble into chalky stars,
constant, silent, as the poles;
over a stone, broad as a bed,
a wiry blackbird stares and stares,
its yellow eye, exacting, dumb,
illuminating nothing. Here,
in the world of worms and birds,
near all these animals we've named,
no saving word replies. Maybe

there is no saving. Time
will run its slick seam through our sheet,
the sturdy, ceaseless ticking,
true to its dimension, ending
always in a silent fray
above somebody's feet.
Like all these hand-mocked, moss-choked stones

Eli   *Nahum*   *Noble*   *Gad*

Patience *Comfort*   *Hope*   *Relief*

it ends but does not move.

§

I'm trying to imagine life for both of you:
how in the broad blank rooms of Death his house,
perhaps, although I know it isn't true,
you come to a beginning once again—
the hairy plaster cracking off the ribs,
the sockets lightless, every joint undone,
yet pushing through the buckled sill, new grass,
and in the broken hearth a rush of birds.

These bodies, that corrupted fell,
Shall uncorrupted rise, (life,
And mortal forms shall spring to
Immortal

§

But doors are closing against the world.
It's late, it's always been too late,
and everyone's an infant now, now
or very, very soon, speechless
as the rubbed-out stones,
engraved beyond engraving.

When mellancholly in soft silence reigns
And the rank grass waves o'er the cheerless ground

The horizon's O is burning into black.
Somewhere marries nowhere.
The stones divorce the words.

III

After Visiting Hours

All unnecessary weight is eliminated.... Even the brain cells
needed for song are lost and replaced seasonally in some birds.
–All the Birds of North America, p. 63

At midnight, in the sunroom of the ward,
when you're locked in your pajamas, stupid
with heartbreak, and your throat a frozen stream,
you'll read how birds in winter lose their minds,
or lose that part that urges them to sing—
each glad cell dying in the blood, until
they know no love but the sparse, sterile seed,
the bitter pills that fatten and preserve
their hearts against this thoughtless cold, this dark.
And yet they seem at peace with this: they love,
they turn away from love, they wait for love
to come for them again, and, trusting, sing
the song they knew was gone for good—*I knew*
you'd come back, I knew it, I knew you'd come.

Parables of the Sparrow

Ipso quidem tempore quo intus est, hiemis tempestate non tangitur, sed tamen parvissimo spatio serenetatis ad momentum excurso, mox de hieme in hiemem regrediens, tuis oculis elabitur. Ita haec vita hominum ad modicum apparet; quid autem sequatur, quidve praecesserit, prorsus ignoramus.

For the little while [the sparrow] is inside, the winter blasts can't touch it, but after the briefest moment of peace, it flies away from your sight, out of the storm and then right back into it again. Just this brief is the life of man—and what comes after, or what came before, we just don't know. (Bede)

1.

Think first of all we've meant to you:
how once,

through brightening air, we came, yoked
to Love's car, the dark earth
shivering, our black wings
driving morning forth,

how Kythereia, foam-born
goddess, called by her faithful, lover
of genitals, sweetly laughed,
her voice a seed blown over the sea,
over the sun-blind ruins,
and how, as hyacinth,
your eyes bloomed.

2.

Or: perched on your lover's breast,
pecking tender fingers, lips,
loved by her more than she loved her eyes,
both nothing and all, a miracle.

3.

How later we were falling,
compared to numbered hairs.
Every sparrow different,
according to your tale, but really
there was only ever one,
a symbol dropping manna-like,
a known thing in a world of loss.
Ages now, we have been your consolation.

4.

Just so, tonight, caught up among
your helpless ealdormen and thegns,
each thickening minute diminishing
your scope, the dim and twisting snow
encircling you like walls of ash,
you call me up again in your distress,
and lay my little spine out like a book,

and read, how yesterday,

after the storm, the ice
was falling from the trees.
A little breeze
stirred the minor
chiming in the limbs, first,
precious as the skin-thin
rims of goblets, then
as horses
punishing the ground,
pure sound, loud over loud.
I tell you this in words
you understand.

Then, in the after-silence,
a few low birds
sat quarreling in the thyme;
beyond the stile, the roebuck
barked and leapt away. Night
fell open again,
the hooked moon
pinning itself in the pocked sky.

After dark, the usual threats—
the moon-faced owl
stalked the air,
the barn-cat shook the weeds.
On the trees and on the grass,
the hoarfrost lay
its mean little rime; here and there
a field-mouse gasped
as beak and claw tucked in.

Then, much later,
snow. The moon
went dark, and awkward
whiteness tumbled down,
settling
on the limbs like lime.
I flew for shelter then,
and found the smoke-hole of your hall.
How bright, how hard
you looked: the women
nursing the young, their red
heads flushed in the hearth-light,
the old men curled on tiny stools,
a few dogs nodding on skins.

§ 58

You were gathered in your cups
by then, lost to each other. Stranger
and stranger you grew to me, I could not
put you together, and then
as soon, it seemed, as I'd come in,
I was caught up in the smoke again,
then in the snow, then lost.
Tomorrow will be much the same,
more wind, more water and light.

I cannot say how you belong to this.
You tell me what I mean.

The Oldest Word Carved into the Oldest Stone

In a field, in New Hampshire, the forsythia
sings in the April snow, its gold tongues
chanting in idiot praise, all wholly

unafraid of life, of death, possessing
the clear courage of the infant
born without a brain, or shining

fanatic, blinkered mule, incapable
of wondering what greater
crimes we might yet be

capable of forcing on our own, yet singing
always, only, always, again, *Gloria,*
only *Gloria Deo* without end,

until each slim tongue becomes a sail full of the world,
and each thin leaf is carved into the world
like the oldest word carved into the oldest stone.

§

Frost blackens the mouth of every bud.
Judas is falling on his field of blood.
Christ again on his bare tree is bowing

under the equinox, where now are crossed
both butchers and their meek, tissue and tear,
cataract, eye, we watch them meet and change,

dumb, brilliant, the burning snow, betraying
the newblown seed, a tumor, nursing
under the ribs its rich maternal blood,

delicate, clean as the third thumb,
graceful as the killing fluid
dancing through the brain,

patterning out its wordless praise—O foot
of the whirlwind, point of the bone, first
breach of the innocent vein—how

can we sing through this, the faltering flesh,
burning back to the zero bone again,
the thoughtless amens of that gold choir?

The oldest word is *finished,* or *forsaken,* or *forgive.*
Christ dies again beneath the equinox and still
this world is not our home.

Triptych

I. Kosovo

It should be a day
   in March, or April,
      when the first blue flowers

force their infant heads,
   when the sunshine
      lashes the black

tree-trunks, and the bare
   limbs flail
      in the sweet, raw wind.

The day should be
   so perfect, so true, that do
      what you will, you will be

unable to add
   a single detail.
      No one will notice

the meandering blood
   in the bright grass,
      not even the shrill birds

who will continue
   praising perfect spring
      well into the dark.

II. Kigali

And here the boys, half-drunk on warm
    banana beer, sweating gold, their sweating mass-
        produced machetes whispering rhythmically, kill

the old women with their granddaughters now,
    the technique identical
        to that of other dreamers, one quick

downward arc, introducing the blade below
    the knotted mandible, across the bleating
        windpipe, like praying, fucking, another

inherited desire, one of several ways
    of chasing after wind, releasing
        breath from body, a gesture

impossible to forget, always
    again, we remember,
        and of course we have memorials.

III. Arlington, April 2003

    dedicate, we cannot
    consecrate, we cannot

All night the city quivers and is green,
    a deep-sea dream replaying on TV.
        Again the bombs (again) sink down like stones.

Then, on the bottom, the soldiers swim
    in camouflage (as harlequins)
        across the theatre's toy stage,

their faces motley, blackened under masks,
    as turtles, hatchling hellbenders, their tasks,
      it seems, so native to their final nerve,

tuned to a single impulse; out to die, to kill,
    they swarm the crescent, flood and spill
      the currents of blood and seed,

while leagues away the marble eyes
    of Lincoln stare. His hands are cold.
      He grips his chair. He will not rise.

Res Publica

after a tyrant

We will insist that he deserved this fate,
lying unwept and disarrayed in state,
proclaim the dirt packed in his mouth was just
if hard, he suffered what he gave, and must
lie down at last among our common things,
teeth and fillings, our shoes and wedding rings,
yet never say mere blood, below his myth, had rushed,
obedient and blind; he was like us.

After a Wake

Let all the mourners let you be
    alone with your lover;
let all the weak light quietly
    retreat, under cover

of earth, or sheet, or cinder-cloud,
    and let him come, possess
your bones, and blood, and pray aloud
    for endless pain, endless

desire, though it tear your breast, pray
    for death's mercy and cry,
"All things are born and pass away,
    but suffer me to lie

awhile with my own fair sorrow,
    let him not also die."
Pray still, when you wake tomorrow,
    that time shall not deprive

you of your comfort and distress.
    Pray that he never leave,
or fall into forgetfulness.
    Pray that you always grieve.

Widow's Magnificat

It was quick, a cloud canceling the sun. Early April, the air a warm rush. Just weeks later, visiting his grave, I found the grass already tousled and lush, long as grief. I thought, excess too is a form of mourning.

§

People will teach you about pity. I was still young, one drunk man said: "Young as Michelangelo's Mary."

§

In the bowl, sugar lingers. You notice this, how quickly objects shed their transience, come forward to fill the vacancy.

§

The day I finally changed the sheets, I stood at the window a long time. The yard was dark with summer, almost black. I was older now, the world was older, and he did not know it. Outside, a squirrel perched on his bicycle, orating to no one. I thought of the squirrel's heart, quickly, quietly beating, the dumb nub pushing out life. In the kitchen the radio was on, and the voice meant nothing to me: two stones clicking together, a valve opening, snapping shut. One day you are given the world's heaviest book and told that you must carry it. When you open it, you find the pages blank. Click, shut.

§

Later I decided it was a lie: there is no heartbreak, the heart will bite but cannot feel. My heart, a cur that will not heel, cornering me in this room.

§

Up late reading, three moths thumping on the light. Midway through, I find the page turned down where he left off. The heroine has just made her big decision, mailed a letter, boarded a train. How easily they shed their continents, these women. Entire strata, bedrock, gravel, the wormy earth, whole water tables shrugged off like silk shawls, hors d'oeuvres politely refused. How easily she puts her foot on that step, reaches up gracefully, a touch self-consciously, to accept the conductor's hand. There is very little reality in the world. Even the moths are deceived.

§

Waking, a strange old line snags in my ear: *Woman, what have I to do with thee?* Just before dawn, the first cold wind of the season washes through the screen. I am a twig, a torn wet root. Where is God's eye?

As a child, lost in Boston, I stepped into a church in the middle of a snowstorm, my skin hot with frost. In the back pews, medieval vagrants hunkered in their rags. Far off, the priest gestured mysteriously in semaphore, a black dot in a viewfinder. I recall now that the gospels disagree here: *Blessed are you poor./ Blessed are the poor in spirit.* When pressed, we will admit that salvation is a mighty thing. Let us warm up first.

§

A strange phrase, *mortification of the flesh.* But this morning the
living body horrifies me more than the corpse. His body, the
smooth long limbs, so long loved, now corrupted, corrupted past
corruption, given over wholly to the strangeness of clay. My body,
still trapped in wanting, alone in this bed. You will have seen how
a grave can disturb us with its demands. It wants to be covered, to
be kept clean, to be marked like a bride is marked, but most of all,
to have the body of another. I get up, make coffee, feel humiliated.
When people say *I want to die,* this is part of what they mean.

§

On Christmas Eve he came to me in a dream. Smaller, with a nose
he'd never had in life; one eye had turned from green to almost
black, and his clothes, too, seemed borrowed, stiff, those of a
lunatic or fugitive. He stood behind the steam-pipe, elbows
drawn in, a baby bird shaking blue fingers. His lips shivered.
It was terrifying beyond consolation, the thought that he had
been lost out there in the world's weather. I asked him, lamely,
What can I get you? He didn't speak, and I wondered then if even he
knew where he was, or what. His thin bones clacked like a cracked
toy, and I thought, this is not my husband. But he was so true in
other ways, his wrists, his crooked chin, that I almost felt as though
I ought to let him warm up for a while in bed with me. But I
thought, if I let him in, what will happen then? I was afraid of him,
afraid of being afraid. Stupidly, I said, *Do you want to hear some
records?* But then I remembered that soon after his death, a week in
fact, I'd broken the needle. I was listening to Charlie Parker, the
phone rang, I snapped the needle off the arm. I was hoping he
wouldn't go into the living room and see that, his precious music
so rudely silenced. And he didn't. Nothing happened. We were

frozen there together. I could hear the silence circling the edges of the room, crackling, picking up dust, the weird thumping of something against nothing.

§

Christmas morning now; his family waits downstairs. Upstairs in the bedroom, I am staring out the window again. Swift shadows on the snowcrust, crisp light on the ice. When I was twelve I went skating on a pond five hundred miles away. I was alone, it was below zero, the dusk raw and pearled as an oyster. Everything caught in stillness but me, I remember that exhilaration, the only moving point in the world, my skates carving infinity into the ice. That was the day I started bleeding, I remember the hate I felt, not wanting it, how I had been alone, then not, had escaped from the world then been betrayed. I kept skating, furious, blood darkening my snowsuit, skating an eight, another eight, until it was too black to see, cutting and cutting the same trapped pattern. The pond later melted; the obedient trees bloomed and emptied again and again.

Let it wait. I don't want to go down to them now.

§

They stop in time, the eyes, bright, nervous, hungering for tragedy. One day you walk into a room and no one remembers, someone else has died, married, the eyes follow, you have been freed at last from the plaster. It is almost spring today, the roads half-mud, half-ice, the air breaking open again. In the evening I decide to walk along the river, the smell of new water, new earth, almost visible in the red light. That must have been the ice I heard two days ago, louder than gunshots, whole shelves of ice thundering off the banks to die downstream.

Under a silver beech I am surprised by a snow of tiny feathers.
On a low branch, six feet away, a falcon is devouring a smaller bird,
I think a sparrow. The falcon's beak has split the little bird along
the hinge of its spine, the splayed wings flapping in the breeze.
Minute after minute I watch the falcon's head tug and plunge,
the beak emerging blood-black and slick as a fetus. Later that night,
in bed, I find one of the sparrow's feathers in my hair.

§

Early April, the air a warm rush. He flew into my room last night
and perched on top of the mirror. I had been dreaming about all
my old houses, magically connected in my dream, passing from
one room to another to another. I can't remember what I was
looking for. When I got to the last room, this room, he was here
waiting for me.

When this happens to people, they usually open all the doors and
windows, a traditional symbol of grief. The bird sometimes finds its
way out. Those more desperate turn to brooms. But I knew what I
had to do. I walked across the room to him, softly, and cupped him
in my palms. I don't know the answer to this, if the dead remain
vulnerable as we are, as memory is. But I held him for a moment,
letting the small heart beat warm and quick against my skin.
Then I brought him to the window and let him out.

The Guest

In the woods one winter night I found a throat
half-choked on snow, and thinking it was dead,
was passing, when it coughed—so in my coat
I tucked it home to warm it up in bed.
At dawn it woke me up demanding tea,
then soup and bread, then cigarettes, then rum—
what could I do? Unused to company
in these dark woods so long, my own voice dumb,
I fed it what it asked, and it grew strong,
though as it did it cursed each living thing
for all the wrong it did, and had been done;
and then one morning it began to sing
in tones as sure as stone, and innocent,
I knew it as my own, and sang with it.

Fugue for Crocuses

Though the mountain persists
I confess I've lost the town.
The boy with the angry white hair,
the old sitting-room windows.
Even the flood that obscured the oxbow
in the spring of no sun.
My days? A brown rain,
and the road runs over the house.

Already it is spring in Virginia,
but that is of no account here.
I sleep late in the ice storm,
waking to see the sand trucks out
and crocuses repenting by the door.
What were you doing among the seasons?
Fine crystal moment,
all your blue leaves
poised in a single present.

I sleep again, and know
once you have left this dream
you are gone forever.

Oh, I will try to excavate you
as they try to excavate me.
But what will I find?
Circumstance? No more
than veins in a leaf, blue veins
in the changing waters.

Let the mountain persist.
I will be misled by nothing else.

Want/Not Want

(from the Jataka Tales):

It was the starving-time. A good man and a bad man wandered in the woods. Suddenly, in a clearing ahead, they spied a stag, huge, luminous, good to eat. The bad man shouted "Ahaha!" and drew his bow to kill. The good man, knowing ahimsā paramo dharma *(non-injury the best course) refused to raise his arms against the beast. But it was just an "illusion-stag," and the bad man's arrows fell in vain.*

A day later, fire broke out in the woods. The good man and the bad man fled in terror, coming at last to a raging river too wild to get across. At that moment the illusion-stag reappeared to ferry the good man, only the good man, across the river, leaving the bad man to perish horribly in the flames.

A noblewoman asked her confessor
how to attain salvation.
He said, You have to love God.

She asked, what if I want
to love God? Is that enough?

> Simone Weil changed her handwriting.
> Her letters unmade themselves until
> they became as pure as undressed stones.
> She hated dancing, hated being kissed.
> Her capital O was impregnable.

> > The word *Sanskrit* means adorned, finished.
> > I wanted to know everything once, and so
> > I tried to learn it. It was only the start.
> > The script, an ancient centipede,
> > crawled away from me on broken legs.

Yes, he answered, that's enough.

§ 74

She said, what if I want
to want to love God?

It is not that she did not want to eat.
It is that she wanted to starve.

Words, you find, have their desires, too.
They mean, from IE *men-,
hence mens, mentula,
the mind and penis.
They intend, fr. in-tendere,
to stretch out toward,
hence tense, tension.
Vouloir dire, lit., to want to say.

Now her breasts were twins of a gazelle,
her thighs the work of a master craftsman.
Yes, he answered, that's enough.

She'd read once how
Alexander, in solidarity
with his thirsty troops, spilled
his water on the sand. He'd conquered
his desires so he could suffer.
She admired this very much.

The night before my aunt's funeral
I stayed awake till dawn
translating a story from the Jataka tales.
I had to look up every single word.
The sun came up and I was poisoned
with cigarettes and coffee. I'd read
how the good man had mastered his will,
the bad man drawn his bow to kill,
how both went hungry.

What is the lesson here?

Tell him, I am sick of love.
The confessor suffered so badly
blood, the rooster's sign, showed in his seed.
Self-hatred did not dispel it.

> If beauty is excess of meaning,
> and meaning excess of desire,
> then beauty is also excess of desire.
> She liked to smoke, perhaps desiring
> the moment when desire is burned out.
> I find the thought of her smoking beautiful.

> > I'd liked her but I hadn't known her well.
> > I knew she'd been a heroin addict,
> > which is one way of knowing what you want.
> > After she got AIDS she showed me a poem
> > she'd written in her prison writing class,
> > something about one of her old boyfriends
> > taunting her, rubbing his torso at her—
> > See this, baby? Too good. Too good for you.
> > Her teeth were gone by then, her voice a whine.
> > She served me a sandwich on moldy bread
> > and I ate it.

O my love, my dove, my perfect one.
All night his little meaning kept its watch,
a deictic particle indexing
the love which moves the sun and other stars.
He is thinking of writing a theological treatise.

> She dressed plainly, almost like a man.
> People thought she was a saint.
> Saints are almost impossible to define.

§ 76

In the story, the good roots
shriveled and stank.
The women's breasts were beaten
skins, the dry-
mouthed children too sick to cry, and when
they finally came back in
with a couple of wild hens,
all tendon, wracked with mites,
and gave them to the women, they saw
they were filled with tiny stones.
Everything was wood, stone, bone,
the whole world, in a little while
they were to become bone as well.
Her legs had grown so thin she could not stand.

He wants. He does not want
to want. He does not want
to want to want. Et cetera.
He considers Pascal's scourge,
the silence of infinite space.

To mix your ash with God you have to burn.
It's possible to conquer your desires,
but first you have to want to conquer them.

And then they cremated her.
There wasn't much to burn.
I left the church and it was snowing hard,
the world doing what it wanted to do.
I lit a fire that night and watched the flames.
The fire ate, it wanted
what it had eaten,
it was still hungry.

Omega

You were dreaming the end of the world again,
fluttering—the myriad blackbirds, a living smoke

spiraling through dark sun over Patmos—
and this time, waking, you were convinced

that art is the purest form of venery, a coupling
of cruelty with want, there, in those shambles, the crux

where meaning bleeds and is carved into its form, worlds
end, the word, trapped in the mouth, catches

a world already dead, the shutter, blind
to us now, captures only past, just as,

in music, the echo follows what it should precede, and how
lastly, even today this crowded street could end, its air

palpitant for the last time with all its gold and hectoring
flies, shit and meat, the intimate smells,

all the familiar barking of blood and trade,
and all you could say about it is that it was.

For days after, you could not pray, fearing God's
name on your tongue would swallow him,

dead in the pit of your knowing,
the words in your skull arrows piercing

you in silence, dumb-show martyr,
and you wept, knowing yet not knowing

what to do, and that, you realized, was despair.
Then one day, when even the memory of hope had left, you stood

in the empty square, watching the broken fountains
drown in leaves, the ruined houses smoke,

and you did the only thing there was to do,
for you, for all of us: began again, again,

gathering bravely in your fist the chaff,
the dry burnt words to measure absence.

Acknowledgments

Blackbird: "Korē," "Water / Zero"
Boxcar Poetry Review: "In Doubt, Recalling Cordelia," "Omega"
Cerise Press: "Broken Ground"
Long Poem Magazine: "Parables of the Sparrow"
Mimesis: "After Visiting Hours," "A Portrait"
Sahara: "The Collar"
Sonora Review: "Fugue for Crocuses"
Tellus: "Theogony"
The Antioch Review: "Exercises with Fermata"
The Literary Review: "Want / Not Want"
Third Coast: "Lethe," "To His Soon-to-Be Ex-Wife, Imagined as
    a Meadow"
Tidal Basin Review: "Triptych"

*Cover art, "Spirals and Curves," by Jin Choi (jinchoiphotography.com);
author photo by Mary Griffis; cover, interior book design by Diane Kistner
(dkistner@futurecycle.org); Palatino text and titling*

About FutureCycle Press

FutureCycle Press is dedicated to publishing lasting English-language poetry books, chapbooks, and anthologies in both print-on-demand and ebook formats. Founded in 2007 by long-time independent editor/publishers and partners Diane Kistner and Robert S. King, the press incorporated as a nonprofit in 2012. A number of our editors are distinguished poets and writers in their own right, and we have been actively involved in the small press movement going back to the early seventies.

The FutureCycle Poetry Book Prize and honorarium is awarded annually for the best full-length volume of poetry we publish in a calendar year. Introduced in 2013, our Good Works projects are devoted to issues of universal significance, with all proceeds donated to a related worthy cause. Our Selected Poems series highlights contemporary poets with a substantial body of work to their credit.

We are dedicated to giving all of the authors we publish the care their work deserves, making our catalog of titles the most diverse and distinguished it can be, and paying forward any earnings to fund more great books.

We've learned a few things about independent publishing over the years. We've also evolved a unique, resilient publishing model that allows us to focus mainly on vetting and preserving for posterity the most books of exceptional quality without becoming overwhelmed with bookkeeping and mailing, fund-raising activities, or taxing editorial and production "bubbles." To find out more about what we are doing, come see us at www.futurecycle.org.

The FutureCycle Poetry Book Prize

All full-length volumes of poetry published by FutureCycle Press in a given calendar year are considered for the annual FutureCycle Poetry Book Prize. This allows us to consider each submission on its own merits, outside of the context of a contest. Too, the judges see the finished book, which will have benefitted from the beautiful book design and strong editorial gloss we are famous for.

The book ranked the best in judging is announced as the prize-winner in the subsequent year. There is no fixed monetary award; instead, the winning poet receives an honorarium of 20% of the total net royalties from all poetry books and chapbooks the press sold online in the year the winning book was published. The winner is also accorded the honor of being on the panel of judges for the next year's competition.